GW01605137

Published 1983 by
The Hamlyn Publishing Group Limited
London · New York · Sydney · Toronto
Astronaut House, Feltham, Middlesex, England

ISBN 0 600 38849 2

These stories first appeared in *The Enid Blyton Pennant Series* published in 1950 by Macmillan & Co. Limited.

Printed in Italy

The Magic Mirror
and other stories

Enid Blyton

Illustrated by Val Biro

Hamlyn

London · New York · Sydney · Toronto

Contents

The magic mirror

'Sammy, don't frown like that!' said Mother. 'It makes you look so ugly.'

Sammy looked up. His mother thought he looked a very ugly little boy. His forehead was wrinkled like an old man's, and the corners of his mouth were turned down.

'I can't think why you are always frowning,' said Mother. 'You ought to be cheerful and good-tempered, not gloomy and snappy, as you so often are. I don't know what you will be like when you are grown up!'

'I shall be all right,' said Sammy, crossly.

'You won't,' said Mother. 'You make your grown-up face whilst you are still a child, you know. I think you will be an ugly, cross man! Do cheer up, Sammy, and smile a bit, and be kind and jolly, instead of such a little cross-patch.'

Sammy didn't believe his mother when she said that children made the faces they would have when they were grown-up. He thought that was silly. But it wasn't. It was quite true.

One day he met Old Man Blue-Eyes. He was a strange old fellow, with eyes as blue as the sky, a jolly red face, and a mouth that was always smiling. Everyone liked Old Man Blue-Eyes. Sammy did, because he was so merry and bright.

'Hallo, hallo!' said Old Man Blue-Eyes, stopping by Sammy. 'Still the same old frown, still the same old sulky mouth! My word, you'll be an ugly old man one day!'

'My mother says that sort of thing too,' said Sammy. 'She says that children make their grown-up faces whilst they are still children. But they don't, do they?'

'Of course they do!' said Old Man Blue-Eyes. 'Now Sammy, you come home with me for a minute or two, and I'll let you have a look in my magic mirror. Then you'll see that what your mother says is true. You do make your own face!'

A magic mirror! That sounded fine. Sammy trotted along with Old Man Blue-Eyes feeling excited. The old man took him into his neat and tidy little cottage, and pointed to a dark wall. A curious mirror shone there, perfectly round, set in a shining silver frame.

'Now you go and look at yourself there whilst I talk to you,' said Old Man Blue-Eyes. 'Go along. You'll see something strange.'

So Sammy went and stood in front of the mirror. At first he could see nothing for there seemed a kind of moving mist in the glass. Then it cleared, and he saw his own face.

'Look at your face now,' said Old Man Blue-Eyes. 'It could be a nice face, for it has big brown eyes, a generous sort of mouth, a straight nose, and nice wavy hair round it.'

That was true. Sammy might have been quite a nice-looking boy if he hadn't frowned and sulked so much. He stared at his own face, and the old man went on talking quietly and sadly.

'Now see that frown on your forehead – see the wrinkles it makes, and the nasty little straight lines between your eyes – look at your mouth, turned down in a sulky way – see how gloomy those nice brown eyes look! Now watch!'

A mist came into the magic mirror again and for a few moments Sammy could see nothing. Then it cleared, and he had a shock. He was still looking at himself – but he was much older!

'Here we are again,' said Old Man Blue-Eyes. 'Ten years older – a big boy, growing up. Unpleasant fellow he looks, doesn't he?'

He did! He looked cross and unfriendly. Sammy didn't like the look of him at all.

'See those frown-wrinkles there?' said Old Man Blue-Eyes. 'Worse than ever, aren't they? They make that boy look quite old! And did you ever see such an ugly mouth? I shouldn't think that boy has any friends, would you?'

'No,' said Sammy. 'I don't much like the look of him. It isn't me, is it?'

Old Man Blue-Eyes didn't answer. A mist came into the mirror again, and Sammy stared hard. What was coming next?

It cleared away, and another face looked out. It was the face of a grown man. Sammy hated it. It was a hard, miserable face, and the forehead was wrinkled all over.

'Look at those wrinkles and the little lines between the eyes, the ones we make when we frown hard,' said Old Man Blue-Eyes. 'Don't they make this man's face ugly? And look at his mouth – see the lines that run from his nose to his chin, and make him look so hard and old! I think he is a nasty fellow, don't you agree?'

'I don't want to see any more,' said Sammy, frightened, for the man was very like him. But the face faded in a new mist, and then, when the mist went, another face was there – the face of a cross, ugly, unhappy old man.

'Here we are again,' said Old Man Blue-Eyes. 'What a poor miserable, bad-tempered old fellow! He has no friends to love him, and he loves no one, not even a dog. How I do pity him, don't you?'

'Yes,' said Sammy, in a low voice. 'I don't want to be like that. This mirror frightens me! Old Man Blue-Eyes, the people in the mirror aren't really me when I'm grown-up, are they?'

'I'm afraid so,' said Old Man Blue-Eyes, in a sad voice. 'We make our own faces, and we make our own lives, happy or unhappy. Didn't you see the frown-wrinkles and the sulky lines in those faces – just the same as you have now? Well, they grow, of course. It's a pity, Sammy – you could be a nice little boy if you liked.'

Sammy slipped away without a word. He was very upset. He simply couldn't grow up like that! But what was he going to do about it? He went to look into his own mirror at home.

'I'll just smile, and see if that makes me any different,' he thought. So he smiled. And oh, what a nice-looking little boy he saw in the

mirror, what a kind little child! His eyes creased at the corners and were merry and bright, his mouth turned up, his wrinkles went.

'I'm the sort of boy people would want to be friends with,' thought Sammy, in surprise. 'I'm not going to frown or sulk any more. I won't be ugly. I won't be cross. I won't grow up into that ugly, miserable old man I saw in the magic mirror!'

So he stopped frowning and smiled instead. He laughed instead of grumbling. He was friendly, and soon he had plenty of friends.

Did you know that we make our own faces? We can be just what we want to be, so go and look in the mirror once or twice, and make up your mind what face you want to grow – a kind and smiling one, or a cross and frowning one. You can choose for yourself.

The grand doll

There was once a very grand doll, dressed just like a king. He had a golden crown on his head, and a red cloak that flowed out round him.

He was very grand indeed, and he thought a lot of himself. He sat in the toy-shop and spoke to the other toys.

'I shall soon be bought and taken to a lovely home. I shall be king of all the toys there. I shall rule them, and make them bow down to me.'

So, when he was bought, and taken to a fine home full of toys, he was pleased. He looked round at the dolls and animals, and spoke in a high and mighty voice.

'Good evening! I am king-doll. Do you see my golden crown? I shall

rule over you and be your king.'

Nobody said anything. The clock-work mouse gave a little giggle, and the king-doll glared at him.

'Did you all hear what I said? I am your king, and you are lucky to have me.'

'Well, we don't want you,' said the sailor-doll. 'We have a queen, and we don't want a king.'

'Where's your queen?' said the king-doll, looking all round for a doll that wore a crown and looked as grand as he did. But he didn't see one.

'This is our queen,' said the sailor-doll, and he took the arm of a dear little doll, with a kind face, a plain red frock, and two golden plaits. She smiled, and her eyes looked kind.

'What a funny sort of queen to have!' said the king-doll, and he laughed unkindly. 'Not at all pretty – dressed in an old red frock – not even a crown on her head! And she looks rather stupid too.'

'Don't talk of our queen like that!'

squeaked the clockwork mouse, crossly. 'I shall bite you if you do.'

'No, no,' said the queen-doll. 'You mustn't speak like that, Mouse. You know I have never wanted to be your queen. You must have this fine doll for your king – he looks very grand.'

'Well – he can be king too, and we'll see how he gets on,' said the clown. The king-doll was pleased. He set his crown quite straight, and looked round for a throne.

He chose a pretty chair and made the sailor-doll fetch a cushion or two out of the dolls' house for him to sit on.

'Now you shall all practise your bows,' he said. 'People have to bow to kings. And you must each think of a nice present to give me.'

But nobody came to bow, and nobody gave him a present. Instead they went to the queen-doll, who was sewing, and she told them a story.

Nobody paid much attention to the grand king-doll. Nobody seemed even to want to talk to him, or hear his tales of the toy-shop and all he did there. He was so cross because the clockwork mouse giggled at him that he smacked him hard, and the little mouse went crying to the queen-doll.

She gave him a blue ribbon to tie round his neck, so he soon stopped crying. The king-doll looked across at the little queen-doll, with her golden plaits.

'She's always busy at something,' he thought crossly. 'Kings and queens oughtn't to work hard, as she does. Whatever does she do all the time?'

Sometimes she mended the clown's coat, which was always

getting torn. Once she sewed up a hole in the teddy bear. He had caught himself on a nail, and his sawdust was leaking out. It frightened him, so the queen-doll sewed up the hole and made him all right again.

The queen-doll settled quarrels too. Sometimes the teddy bear fought the clown, and then the queen-doll stopped them, and made them say they were sorry. She took the clockwork mouse on her knee and was kind to him when somebody trod on his tail, which very often happened.

'Good gracious, she's nothing more than a silly little mother to all the toys!' said the king-doll to himself in great disgust. 'Wasting her time like that! Why doesn't she make the toys work for her, and sew her a beautiful dress and cloak instead of that old red dress? Why doesn't she make them say "Your Majesty" and bow to her when they speak?'

When a week had gone by the king-doll called a meeting of the toys, and he spoke to them in his grand, high-and-mighty voice.

'Toys! I have watched you for a week, and I want to tell you that your queen-doll is not a queen at all. She just acts like a silly little mother, fussing over you, and working hard instead of making you fuss over her

and work for her. It's all wrong. She doesn't know how to be a queen. But I know how to be a king! So why don't you choose me, and have a king instead of a queen. I'd be a king you could be proud of.'

'Pooh!' said the clown, rudely. 'We'd never be proud of you! You're dreadful! You're vain and selfish and lazy!'

'We want someone to love and someone who loves us,' squeaked the clockwork mouse. 'That's the best sort of ruler to have – somebody like ourselves, but kinder and wiser, who understands us, and loves us and wants us to be happy. You would be a bad king!'

'Be quiet!' said the king-doll, crossly.

'I don't really want to be queen,' said the little doll with golden plaits, smiling at the king-doll. 'I don't feel a queen. You can be king if you want to, but let me still love the toys and look after them.'

The king-doll suddenly felt ashamed of himself. He knew the queen-doll was better and wiser and kinder than he would ever be. He knew that he was vain and lazy and selfish, just as the clown had said. He loved the little queen-doll, and

he wanted her to love him too, just as she loved the other toys. He realised what he should do.

He took off his golden crown and set it on the little doll's golden head. He took off his red cloak and put it gently round her shoulders.

'There!' he said. 'Now you are a real queen. 'My queen, as well. I should never make as good a king as you are a queen. I will be an ordinary doll, and love you as the others do. I can see that you are queen of all our hearts, as well as

queen of the play-room!'

Well, wasn't that nice of him? All the toys cheered loudly, and the little queen-doll went red with delight. To think she had a crown and a cloak! Dear dear, whatever would happen next?

The king-doll kept his word. He was just an ordinary doll, and he loved the little queen, and did everything he could for her. And one day I think the toys will really make him their king – but he will have earned a crown and cloak then, and that is the best way for him to get them, isn't it?

The dog that remembered

Peter was such a lucky boy. Nice things were always happening to him.

'My uncle is taking me to the circus!' he would say to the other children. Or, 'My Auntie is giving me a tricycle! Think of that!'

When he was ill his Granny took him his favourite jellies. They were nice jellies, the top half pink and the lower half yellow. His Grandpa sent him a fine jigsaw puzzle that made a wonderful steamer when it was all fitted together.

Once when he fell into the river a bigger boy jumped in and saved him. The big boy got his clothes wet and spoilt his new tie, but he didn't make a fuss about that. He was glad to have saved Peter.

But Peter never seemed grateful for anything, and sometimes he didn't even remember to say thank you. His mother used to worry about this.

'You are such a lucky little boy, Peter,' she said. 'You have so many nice things given to you, and so

many lovely treats. People are so kind to you when you are ill – and if you are in trouble they always help you. But you never seem to remember their kindness.'

'Don't I?' said Peter, in surprise. 'How ought I to remember their kindness then?'

'Well, Granny was good to you when you were ill, and you should go and see her more often, and take her some flowers from your garden,' said his mother. 'And that boy who dived in and saved you from the river – you never even went to see if his clothes had dried all right. You didn't even offer to buy him a new tie when you knew his own had been quite spoilt. And you had plenty of money in your money-box.'

'Oh,' said Peter. 'I didn't think.'

'Well, you ought to think,' said his mother. 'I keep thinking for you, but it's not the same thing.'

Now one day when Peter was out in the woods, he heard a dog whining in pain. He looked about and soon found a little puppy whose foot had been caught in a rabbit-trap.

'Poor thing!' said Peter. 'I'll set you free – and I'll throw the trap away so that it can never catch and hurt any animal so cruelly again!'

He knew how to open the trap. Soon the dog was free. It licked its paw, still whining. It licked Peter's hand too, and looked up at him out of grateful brown eyes.

'Poor fellow!' said Peter, patting

him. 'I'm glad I came along. Go home, and get your foot seen to.'

The dog went off, limping on three legs, holding its hurt paw up in the air. It still whined, for it was in pain.

The next day the dog appeared outside Peter's home. Its hurt foot was neatly bound up, and Peter was glad. He looked at the dog and the dog looked at him.

'Woof,' said the dog, and licked Peter's hand.

'He has come to say thank you,' said Peter's mother. 'Isn't that good of him?'

The dog trotted away again. It was back the next day, and this time it brought a big bone in its mouth. It waited till Peter came out, and then it ran to him and laid the bone at his feet.

'Oh Mother, look! The dog has brought me its bone!' cried Peter. 'Dear old dog – I don't want your bone, but thank you for bringing it!'

A week later Peter was running through the woods when a tramp stepped out from some bushes. 'Hi, wait!' said the tramp. 'Have you any money? If you have, you must give it to me!'

Peter was frightened. He had two ten pence pieces and he didn't want to give them to this rough man. He tried to slip away but the tramp caught him.

'Now then!' he said, and gave Peter a slap on the cheek. 'Don't you try to run away! You give me your money!'

'Help! Help!' cried Peter, trying to get away. But there was no one in the woods that day. The tramp shook the boy hard, and Peter almost fell over.

Then through the woods there came the pattering of feet, and the dog ran up. He still ran on three paws, for the fourth one hurt him.

He leapt at the tramp with a fierce growl. The man let go of Peter at once and put up his hands to defend himself.

'Call him off, call him off!' he said. 'Don't let him bite me!'

But the dog nipped him well at the back of the leg, and the tramp fled through the woods, howling. Peter sat down, trembling. The dog sat close by him, licking him every now and again, looking up at him out of big brown eyes.

'Woof,' he said. Peter put his arm round him. 'You are a wonderful dog,' he said. 'All I did was to set you free from a trap, and you have never forgotten. You came and thanked me. You gave me a present of a bone you must have badly wanted to eat yourself – and now you have saved me from being robbed by that horrid tramp.'

'Woof,' said the dog, and licked him again.

'Come home with me and let me tell Mother what you have done,' said Peter. So they went home, and Peter told his mother the whole story.

'Isn't he a wonderful dog?' said Peter. His mother nodded.

'Yes,' she said. 'He is better than

a little boy I know! He is grateful – he says thank you – he brings a little present – and he waits for a chance to show how grateful he is, by saving you from that tramp!'

'How funny that a dog should be better than I am!' said Peter, going rather red. 'He keeps on and on remembering the kindness I did to him, doesn't he, Mother? He doesn't forget, like I do. Well, I love him for remembering, and I shall always be friends with him!'

And now Peter too remembers to be grateful when people are kind to him. He is great friends with the dog, and they go for long walks together – but wasn't it funny that a dog had to teach him never to forget a kindness?

The ugly little girl

Katie wasn't very pretty. Her hair was thin and very straight. Her eyes were rather pale. So were her cheeks, because she didn't really get enough good food to eat. She was thin, and because her eyes were weak, she had to wear glasses.

Her clothes were always too big for her or too small, because she had to wear someone else's. They were darned and patched, because Katie's mother was poor, and had a lot of children besides Katie.

When Doreen first went to Katie's school, how she turned up her nose at the ugly little girl! 'Goodness!' she said to Freddie, 'what's she doing at this school? Isn't she ugly? And aren't her clothes dreadful?'

'I like Katie,' said Freddie at once. 'She is coming to tea with me to-day.'

Everyone liked Katie. It was funny, Doreen thought, that anyone should want to be friends with such a poor, badly dressed, ugly little girl. Why was it?

'Katie's kind,' said Alice, when Doreen asked her why she wanted always to sit next to Katie. She asked Jim why he always walked home with Katie instead of with her.

‘Well – Katie’s so kind,’ said Jim.

‘But she’s ugly and all her things are patched and darned,’ said Doreen. ‘I wouldn’t want to be seen walking with Katie.’

‘Those things don’t seem to matter because Katie’s so kind,’ said Ann. ‘I never see her old clothes and plain looks – I just like being with her because she’s so kind.’

'Well, that's just silly,' thought Doreen, puzzled. 'As if kindness could hide things like poor clothes and an ugly face and rats-tail hair! I think Katie is dreadful.'

It was true that Katie was kind. She was always the first to pick up anyone who fell down. She was always the one to take the child in and bathe his hurt knee. Katie often stayed behind to help anyone who had to stay in because their work was bad. Katie never minded helping them.

Katie hadn't a lovely flower-garden at home as some of the children had, so she couldn't bring Miss Brown flowers for the class-room, or fruit for herself.

But that didn't worry Katie. She just went out into the fields and picked bunches of lovely buttercups or sprays of honeysuckle in the woods. She got up early and found mushrooms for Miss Brown, or blackberries.

'You really are a kind little girl,' said Miss Brown.

16

It was Katie who went to see any child who was ill, and took them any poor toy of her own. She didn't mind what she did. She looked after all her little brothers and sisters too, and never spoke crossly to them. They loved her very much.

Nobody seemed to see that Katie was poor and thin and ugly, and not at all nice to look at. Everyone wanted Katie for a friend, everyone asked Katie out to tea, though she could never ask them back, and everyone told her all the things that happened because Katie was a marvellous listener.

All the same Doreen simply could not make herself like Katie. She was ashamed of her. If only she had nicer dresses, or curly hair, or was a bit fatter! But no, Katie stayed as she was, thin and ugly and poor.

Then one day, when Doreen went blackberrying, a horrid thing happened to her. A dog ran at her and barked, and Doreen rushed into the hedge in fright.

Her dress got caught in the brambles, and her arms were dreadfully scratched. The dog went on barking and Doreen screamed, afraid that he was going to bite her.

Someone else was blackberrying there that day, on the other side of the hedge. It was Katie. She heard the scream and scrambled through the hedge at once. 'Why, Doreen,' she said, 'it's you! Don't be afraid of the dog. I'll shoo him away.'

So she did, and the dog ran off. He hadn't meant any harm, really. Doreen was sobbing.

'Look at my nice frock,' she said. 'It's torn here – and here – and look at my poor arms and legs. They are bleeding all over with scratches. And I've upset all my blackberries.'

'Never mind,' said Katie. 'You can have mine. I can get plenty more. You come home with me, and I'll see to your scratches, shall I? I don't live far away.'

It was lovely to have someone speaking so kindly. Doreen went home with Katie, still sobbing. Katie bathed her arms and legs, and bound up one bad scratch. Then she got out a needle and cotton, and mended the tears in Doreen's dress so neatly that you could hardly see the mends at all!

'Oh, thank you,' said Doreen, gratefully. 'You are kind,' Then she gave a scream. 'Oh, Katie! I've lost my brooch – the one Granny gave me for Christmas. Oh, Mother will be so angry with me.'

'We'll look for it as we go home,' said Katie. 'Don't you worry. I'll come back with you and help you to look.'

So they went back, and they looked everywhere for the lovely brooch. And Katie suddenly saw it!

'Here it is,' she said, and she darted to a patch of long grass. 'Yes – I thought I saw something shining. It's your beautiful brooch!'

'Oh, Katie – I'm so pleased,' said Doreen. 'Thank you very much. Now I must go home.'

'Well, take my basket of blackberries with you because you lost all yours,' said Katie. 'I can get some more. Do take them, because you've had such a horrid afternoon!'

She held them out to Doreen, her eyes shining kindly behind their big glasses. Doreen looked at her –

and dear me, she didn't see a plain, thin, badly-dressed little girl any more! No, she saw Katie, the real Katie, kind and generous and sweet, her kindness shining through her ugliness and poorness, making her beautiful and lovable to see.

'You are a dear, Katie,' said Doreen. 'I do like you. Will you be my friend? Please do. And will you come to tea to-morrow?'

Katie looked surprised. 'Why, I always thought you didn't like me,' she said, and she smiled. 'I'm glad you do. I know I'm not much to look at, and I'm always so glad when anyone likes me.'

'You're the nicest girl in the school,' said Doreen and she meant it. 'I don't know why I didn't think so before!'

And the next day Doreen didn't notice Katie's straight hair and thick glasses and poor dress – all she saw was kind little Katie, whom everyone loved.

The funny thing was, when a new boy came to school and said to Doreen, 'What a dreadful child that Katie-girl looks!' Doreen was very cross.

'What do you mean?' she said. 'I like Katie. Katie's kind.'

That's what I would like to have said of me – wouldn't you?

The frisky little goat

It had been raining very hard, but now the sun looked as if it was just coming out.

Jack stood at the window and wished he could go out. He wanted to see if there were any blackberries ripe. He felt as if he could eat about a hundred nice juicy ones.

'Mummy, can I go out?' he called.

'No,' said Mummy. 'It's too wet. There are great big puddles everywhere, and the grass is soaking.'

'I do want to go out,' said Jack. 'I want to see if there are any blackberries.'

'You heard what I said,' said Mummy. So Jack didn't say any more. He went on looking out of the window, wishing and wishing that he was out with the ducks. They liked the wet. They splashed through all the puddles and had a lovely time.

Someone came to see his mother. They went into the drawing-room and shut the door. Jack stayed still, thinking hard.

He could slip out whilst his mother was talking. It was Mrs. Jones who had come, and she always stayed a very long time. He could go to the field where the blackberries grew, pick some, and then slip back before his mother knew. It would be fun, he thought, to run in and out without anyone knowing.

Jack was not a very obedient little boy. He often disobeyed his mother, and she got very cross with him. He knew he ought not to disobey now – but he did so badly want those blackberries.

'I won't go into any puddles. I'll try not to get into the long wet grass,' he thought. 'Then I shan't get my feet wet.'

He slipped out of the garden door. He went across the garden, taking care not to tread in any puddles. He only had on his brown sandals, so he had to be very careful indeed.

He came to the field and climbed over the gate. Then down he jumped and made his way to the hedge where the blackberries grew.

He didn't see a frisky little nanny-goat in the field. But the nanny-goat saw him. Ha, a little boy to play with! That was nice.

The goat trotted up to Jack and bleated. It made him jump. He turned round and saw the goat. He was afraid of goats.

'Go away,' he said, but the goat didn't go away. It stood there bleating. Then it skipped high in the air, put down its head and butted Jack lightly on the legs.

'Don't!' said Jack, in fright, and tried to run away. But the goat thought the little boy was playing a game with it, and it was full of joy and liveliness.

It ran playfully at Jack, and he screamed. He ran as fast as his legs would take him, and the goat skipped behind him, butting him every now and again.

Jack splashed through enormous puddles. He stumbled over muddy patches and splashed his legs with mud up to the knees. He cried big tears all down his cheeks.

The goat wouldn't let him get over the gate. It frisked round him, and every time he tried to climb up, the goat butted him down.

Jack saw a gap in the hedge and ran for that. But the goat was there first. Jack ran another way, and the goat ran after him, enjoying the game very much. It thought the little boy was a fine play-mate.

The goat butted Jack a bit harder, and he fell into an enormous puddle. He was soaked from head to foot! Whatever would his mother say!

Somehow he managed to scramble through the gap. But, of course, the goat went through after him too! So there was Jack, racing for his house, with the goat skipping and tripping all round him!

Jack rushed in through the door, and the goat rushed in too. His mother was just coming into the hall, holding Jack's rubber boots in her hand.

She stared in great surprise at Jack and the goat. 'Whatever are you and the goat doing?' she said, and she shooed the goat out of the door. It went back to its field, pleased to have had such a fine game.

'Jack! Where have you been? Whatever have you been doing to yourself?' said his mother. 'Look at your sandals soaked through – and your socks – and all your clothes muddy and torn. What have you been doing?'

'I went to get some blackberries,' wept Jack.

'Then you are a naughty, disobedient little boy,' said Mummy, crossly. 'I told you it was too wet. Now see what has happened to you!'

'The goat chased me,' sobbed Jack. 'It chased me home!'

'It wouldn't have chased you if you hadn't disobeyed me and gone out,' said Mummy. 'And see – I had just gone to get your rubber boots for you, and I was going to tell you to put them on, and go and find some blackberries! If you had obeyed me, you would still have been indoors, and could have put on your boots and gone out.'

'The goat would still have chased me,' said Jack.

'No, it wouldn't,' said Mummy. 'because I should have told you not to go into that field. It is only a playful little thing, anyway – it couldn't do you much harm if you were sensible and didn't run away and fall over.'

'I'm sorry, Mummy,' said Jack.

'So am I,' said Mummy. 'Sorrier than you because now that you have spoilt your clothes, you can't go out to tea this afternoon. Your other jerseys are being washed – this is the only one you have clean, and now it is wet and dirty and torn.'

'I didn't know I was to go out to tea,' said Jack.

'Well, Mrs. Jones came to ask if you could go to a party with her little grandson,' said Mummy. 'Now you won't be able to go. Well – you shouldn't have been disobedient. Until you learn to be sensible and obey, you will find things often go wrong. You had better go upstairs now and get washed!'

Jack was silly, wasn't he? If he hadn't disobeyed, he could have put on his rubber boots, played with the goat instead of running away, and had a lovely time at the party. Perhaps he will be more sensible another time!

Lucy Lively and Dicky Dull

Lucy Lively lived next door to Dicky Dull. She was always trying to be friends with him, but it was very hard work indeed.

'Come over and let's play Red Indians!' Lucy would say. But Dicky Dull wouldn't want to. 'It's too hot,' he would say.

Another time Lucy would call over the wall and ask Dicky to come for a walk.

'No, it's too cold,' Dicky would call back.

'Well – come indoors and do a jigsaw with me – or I've got some puzzles in a book you might like. They are great fun to do – riddles and things, you know,' said Lucy.

'Oh, that's too hard,' said Dicky. 'I hate having to think hard, Lucy. It's bad enough at school.'

'What a dull fellow you are – your brain is too dull to have fun over puzzles, your legs are too dull to go for a walk – no wonder you haven't any friends, Dicky Dull!'

'You are very lucky to have so many,' said Dicky. 'You are always going out to tea and having fun. I am always at home by myself.'

'Well, you come out to-morrow with me,' said Lucy. 'My aunt is having a party. It will be such fun. She said I could take a friend.'

So Dicky Dull went. But he wouldn't join in the blind man's buff and he was never quick enough to get rid of the slipper when he had it, in the game 'Hunt the Slipper'.

Lucy played every game, and laughed and enjoyed herself. She won at musical chairs, and she was never caught at Blind Man's Buff. People liked hearing her laugh.

'How that child does enjoy herself!' they said. 'It's nice to see her. What a pity that boy she brought with her doesn't enter into things a bit more. He looks so dull.'

'Cheer up, Dicky!' said Lucy, catching sight of his face. 'Enjoy yourself whilst you can – the party will soon be over.'

Before the party ended, two or three children asked Lucy to come to their parties too. She was such a jolly, lively little girl. She made people laugh and feel cheerful.

Dicky was sulky on the way home, when Lucy told him of the parties she had been asked to. 'I wasn't asked,' he said. 'You get all the luck.'

When the summer time came, it was just the same. Lucy took Dick to a picnic. There were about seven children and two grown-ups. Dicky soon grumbled because they had to walk quite a long way.

'I shall be tired before I get there,' he said. 'My legs ache already.'

'Well, what does it matter if you do get a bit tired?' said Lucy, laughing. 'You will enjoy your rest all the more. We're going to have games afterwards, so cheer up, Dicky.'

Dicky wouldn't play games afterwards. He sat looking dull and gloomy. He heard Lucy making jokes and laughing, he saw her helping the smaller ones, and heard her offer to carry something for the grown-ups.

Lucy was the first to see a watching rabbit and the first to hear a robin singing for crumbs. She ran here and skipped there, such a merry, lively, happy little girl that everyone wanted her with them.

'Will you come to my picnic next

week?' Harry said to her. And John asked her to go to the Zoo with him.

'There you are, you see,' said Dicky Dull, miserably. 'Nobody asked me. You have all the luck, Lucy. I wasn't asked to any more picnics, or to go to the Zoo.'

Lucy was sad for Dicky. He looked so miserable. 'Do cheer up,' she said. 'We've had such a lovely picnic, and the games were such fun.'

'I thought it was a horrid picnic, and I hate games like that – having to run and jump,' said Dicky, sulkily.

'Well, you know, Dicky, I think it's your own fault that you don't enjoy things,' said Lucy. 'You won't let your arms and legs join in the fun, you won't let your mind be happy and cheerful so that you can laugh and make jokes. You're dull, dull, dull!'

'No, I'm not – I'm unlucky,' said Dicky, crossly.

'Rubbish!' said Lucy, skipping round him. 'We make our own good or bad luck, my mother always says. You say I have good luck – well, I'm happy and jolly, so people like me with them, they are friends with me, and ask me to go to parties and picnics. That isn't just good luck.'

'Oh,' said Dicky Dull, 'and I suppose you think it's the way I behave that makes people bored with me and not ask me out!'

'Yes, I do,' said Lucy, pleased at having found the reason for Dicky Dull's bad luck. 'So cheer up, Dicky – now you know that you can make your own good or bad luck, you'll be all right! Be happy and jolly and lively, and you'll always have friends and lots of treats!'

What Lucy said was true – but alas, poor Dicky Dull wouldn't believe her. He went on thinking that it was just his bad luck, and he grew duller and duller and duller.

One day he will be a cross, boring old man, so dull that people will hate to go and see him. He will have no children and no grandchildren, but will live alone, grumbling and groaning all day long.

But Lucy – ah, Lucy will be a lively old woman with fifteen grandchildren who love her and see her every week! She will never be alone, and will laugh just as much as ever she did. What a wise and merry old lady she will be, what a lot of presents she will get, and how everyone will love her!

'She's lucky!' old Dicky Dull will groan. 'She always was.'

But she made her own luck, didn't she, she made her own friends and her own happiness! We all do that – and I do hope you are making plenty for yourself.

Little Mister Sly

Mister Sly lived in a small cottage at the edge of Lilac Village. He kept hens, and sold the eggs, but he never gave any away. He was a mean little fellow, and was only generous when he thought he would get something out of it.

Now one day Sly found six eggs that one of his hens had laid away from the hen-house. He felt sure they had been laid weeks ago, because for at least seven weeks he had shut up his hens carefully, and not let them stray.

'What a pity! They will be bad!' he said to himself. 'All wasted!'

Then he thought hard. 'I could give them away. I'll give them to old Mister Little-Nose. He can't smell anything bad or good since he had the flu last year. Maybe he will give me some honey from his bees then.'

So Sly put the eggs into a round basket and took them to Mister Little-Nose.

'Oh, thank you!' said Mister Little-Nose. 'That's kind of you, Sly. I will give you some honey in the summer-time.'

After Sly had gone, Mister Little-Nose heard someone knocking at his door again, and dear me, it was the carrier, bringing twelve eggs for him from his sister.

'Well, well – I've too many eggs now,' he thought. 'I'll send some to the pixie Twinkle.'

So he sent his little servant round to Twinkle with the six eggs that Sly had given him. But before Twinkle could use them she had to leave in a hurry to go and see her aunt, who was ill.

'I'll take the eggs to old Dame Groan,' she thought. 'She's been ill and needs feeding up.'

So she took them to Dame Groan's house and left them outside the door, because Dame Groan was asleep. Twinkle could hear her snoring.

Dame Groan grumbled when she saw the eggs. 'Twinkle might have known that the doctor has said eggs are the one thing I mustn't eat!' she said. 'What a pity! Well, Twinkle is away, so I can't give them back to her. I'll give them to

old Miss Scared. She can do with a bit of good luck, she's so poor.'

Miss Scared was simply delighted with them. 'Oh, thank you, dear Dame Groan,' she said. 'I do hope you are feeling better now. Thank you very much.'

But before Miss Scared could eat any of the eggs, there came another knock at her door. She opened it. Outside stood Mister Sly, a horrid mean look on his face.

'I lent you fifty pence last week,' he said. 'And you said you would pay me sixty pence back this week. Where is the money?'

'Oh, Mister Sly, I haven't got it. Won't you wait till to-morrow?' said Miss Scared. 'Please do.'

'Can't wait,' said Mister Sly.

Then he caught sight of the six eggs. 'Hullo – you've got six eggs! Give me these six eggs, and I'll let you off.'

'All right,' said poor Miss Scared with a sigh, for she had badly wanted an egg for her tea. 'Take them.'

Mister Sly went off with the eggs. He didn't know they were the very same old eggs he had taken to Mister Little-Nose that very morning.

'I'll have bacon and eggs for tea,' he said, and got out his pan. He put in his bacon and it sizzled well. He put in a few mushrooms – and then he cracked an egg on the side of the pan, and let it run in, among the bacon and mushrooms.

But oh dear, it was bad! Mister Sly managed to scrape it out, and tried another egg. That was bad too. They were all bad! The worst of it was that his bacon tasted of bad egg when he ate it, and the whole kitchen smelt dreadful. Mister Sly felt very sick.

He was very, very angry. 'That dreadful Miss Scared!' he said. 'How dare she give me bad eggs!

This is a matter for the police. I will call Mr. Plod in and tell him all about it. He will give Miss Scared a good talking-to, and that will scare her properly.'

So he went to Mr. Plod and told him. Then he and Mr. Plod went to Miss Scared's cottage, and knocked on the door.

'You bad woman! You gave me rotten eggs!' said Sly, angrily. 'Where did you get them from?'

'Oh, Dame Groan sent them to me,' said Miss Scared, as frightened as could be. 'Please, please, don't blame me. I didn't know they were bad. I really didn't.

‘Ha – Dame Groan,’ said Mr. Plod, and wrote the name in his notebook. ‘Come along – we’ll go and see her.’

So they went to Dame Groan. 'Those eggs you gave Miss Scared were bad!' scolded Sly. 'How dare you give away rotten eggs?'

'I didn't know they were bad,' said Dame Groan, in a rage, 'and don't you talk to me like that, Sly.

Twinkle sent me those eggs – she said that Mister Little-Nose had given them to her.'

'We'll go to Mister Little-Nose then,' said Mr. Plod. 'Ah – there he is, just over there! Hi, Little-Nose, I've got something to ask you.'

'What?' said Little-Nose.

'Well, Sly here is trying to trace a batch of bad eggs he had given to him,' said Mr. Plod. 'It seems that Miss Scared gave them to him, and Dame Groan gave them to her, and Twinkle gave them to Dame Groan, and you gave them to Twinkle.

Now – did your hens lay them? And what right have you to send out bad eggs?'

'I've got no hens,' said Mister Little-Nose, in surprise. 'And as for who gave them to me – well, Sly should know, for he sent them round himself!'

'What!' cried Mr. Plod, and snapped his notebook angrily. 'What! Did you give him six bad eggs, Sly? And you have dared to come and complain to me about them and waste my time, when they were your eggs! You must have known they were bad, too. How dare you, I say?'

Sly hadn't a word to say for himself. Little-Nose looked at him in disgust.

'He always was mean,' he said. 'He'd never give away anything good. I might have guessed they were bad. Well, I'm glad they came back to you, Sly, very glad. Serves you right!'

And so it did.